Symbols of American Freedom

The Statue of Liberty

by Hilarie Staton

Series Consultant: Jerry D. Thompson,
Regents Professor of History,
Texas A&M International University

CHELSEA CLUBHOUSE
An Imprint of Chelsea House Publishers

Symbols of American Freedom: The Statue of Liberty

Chelsea Clubhouse
An imprint of Chelsea House Publishers
132 West 31st Street
New York NY 10001

Library of Congress Cataloging-in-Publication Data
Staton, Hilarie.
        The Statue of Liberty / by Hilarie Staton.
            p. cm. — (Symbols of American freedom)
        Includes index.
        ISBN 978-1-60413-516-9
        1. Statue of Liberty (New York, N.Y.)—Juvenile literature. 2. Statue of Liberty
        National Monument (N.Y. and N.J.)—Juvenile literature. 3. New York (N.Y.)—
        Buildings, structures, etc.—Juvenile literature. I. Title. II. Series.
    F128.64.L6S729 2010
    974.7'1—dc22   2009007852

Chelsea Clubhouse books are available at special discounts when purchased in bulk quantities for businesses, associations, institutions, or sales promotions. Please call our Special Sales Department in New York at (212) 967-8800 or (800) 322-8755.

You can find Chelsea Clubhouse on the World Wide Web at http://www.chelseahouse.com

Developed for Chelsea House by RJF Publishing LLC (www.RJFpublishing.com)
Text and cover design by Tammy West/Westgraphix LLC
Maps by Stefan Chabluk
Photo research by Edward A. Thomas
Index by Nila Glikin

Photo Credits: Cover: Shutterstock Images; 5: Glow Images RF/Photolibrary; 6: Library of Congress LC-USZ62-50904; 8: AFP/Getty Images; 12, 32: National Park Service; 13: © North Wind/North Wind Picture Archives; 14, 16, 25, 31, 37: AP/Wide World Photos; 17: Library of Congress LC-USZ62-102634; 18, 22: Getty Images; 23: Library of Congress LC-USZ62-60766; 27: © Bettmann/CORBIS; 28: Edward Moran, Statue of Liberty Enlightening the World, 1886, Museum of the City of New York, The J. Clarence Davies Collection, 34.100.260; 33: Library of Congress LC-USZC4-8050; 35: © JP Laffont/Sygma/Corbis; 39: © Ian Dagnall/Alamy; 40: © Mark L Stephenson/CORBIS; 43: © Alan Schein/zefa/Corbis.

Printed and bound in the United States of America

Bang RJF 10 9 8 7 6 5 4 3 2 1

This book is printed on acid-free paper.

All links and Web addresses were checked and verified to be correct at the time of publication. Because of the dynamic nature of the Web, some addresses and links may have changed since publication and may no longer be valid.

Note: Quotations in the text are used essentially as originally written. In some cases, spelling, punctuation, and the like have been modernized to aid student understanding.

Table of Contents

Words that are defined in the Glossary are in **bold** type
the first time they appear in the text.

Chapter 1

Symbol of Freedom

A huge statue of a woman stands in New York Harbor. She has many names. Frédéric-Auguste Bartholdi, who designed the statue, called her *Liberty Enlightening the World*. She is often called Lady Liberty. Most people know her as the Statue of Liberty.

From its beginning, the statue was a **symbol**. It honored ideas: friendship, freedom, and government by the people (**democracy**). Today, it is still a symbol of these ideas. It is also the symbol of a country—the United States of America—and of the fact that tens of millions of people have come to the United States from all over the world to seek a better life.

The Statue of Liberty is on Liberty Island. This island is in the upper bay of New York Harbor. It is 1½ miles (2½ kilometers) from Manhattan, which is part of New York City. It is less than ½ mile (¾ kilometer) from

New Jersey. The island was known as Bedloe's Island until its name was changed in 1956. The statue faces ships entering the harbor from the Atlantic Ocean. She welcomes people coming to the United States.

The Special Lady

The Statue of Liberty was created in France by Bartholdi, who was helped by Alexandre-Gustave Eiffel. (Eiffel later became world famous for designing the Eiffel Tower in Paris.) The statue was a gift from the French people to the United States to celebrate the 100th anniversary of the

Standing on an island and facing toward the sea, the Statue of Liberty welcomes ships entering New York Harbor.

For immigrants arriving in their new country, the statue was a symbol of hope.

Declaration of Independence. That was the document, approved on July 4, 1776, in which the American colonies declared their independence from Great Britain. The statue honored the long friendship between the United States and France. After the Declaration, France helped the colonists defeat Great Britain and win their independence in the American Revolution. The statue was also meant to remind people of the freedom Americans fought for during the Revolution. To build the statue, Bartholdi and Eiffel used modern and older materials and methods. The result was a beautiful work of art.

Lady Liberty: Movie Star

The Statue of Liberty has appeared in many movies. Some films use it to show that the action is in New York City. In others, like *Ghostbusters II*, the statue comes to life. She helps defeat the villains. In some movies, like *Saboteur* and *X-Men*, people are at the statue itself. Sometimes she is shown in pieces. This often means that the United States or freedom has been destroyed.

Columbia

Colonists in America used Columbia as a symbol. She is a goddess in a flowing gown. Her name comes from Columbus. During the Revolution, she represented the ideas that the American colonists were fighting for. Later, she was used in political cartoons. She was used in World War I posters, but the Statue of Liberty became the more popular symbol. Today, Columbia is seldom used.

The statue was **dedicated** in 1886 (ten years later than originally planned). Millions of people who passed her after that were **immigrants**. An immigrant is a person who moves to a new country to live. In the late 1800s and the early 1900s, more than 12 million immigrants arrived in New York by ship to start a new life in the United States. Most of them had come from Europe and were very poor. For these people, the statue was a symbol of hope—hope for a better life. Many Americans today have grandparents, great-grandparents, or others in their family who passed the statue when they first came to the United States.

About 30 years after the statue arrived, the United States entered World War I in 1917 and sent soldiers to fight in Europe. The U.S. government started to use the Statue of Liberty on posters. Like Uncle Sam and Columbia, it was a symbol that stood for American freedom. All over the country, people saw its picture. Soldiers returning from Europe by ship cheered when they saw this symbol of home.

One hundred years after it opened, the Statue of Liberty was very special to Americans. When it needed to be repaired, many people sent money to help pay for fixing it. Then, there was a huge 100th birthday party for the statue in 1986.

TORCH

CROWN

BOOK

ROBES

SANDALS

CHAINS

The Statue of Liberty itself is a symbol of freedom, and it also has many symbols on it. Originally the torch was not only a symbol but a lighthouse as well.

Symbols on the Statue

Not only is the Statue of Liberty itself a symbol, it also has many symbols on it. She is a tall woman, and her face is calm, but strong. She is dressed in flowing robes and sandals—like the clothing of an ancient Greek goddess. This shows that the democratic government of the United States is based on ideas about democracy that were developed in ancient Greece almost 2,500 years ago.

The statue wears a crown. It has seven spikes—or rays, like rays of the sun. They stand for her ideas shining over the seven continents of the world.

The statue's torch shows she is lighting the way. The light stands for freedom and hope. At first, the statue was also a **lighthouse**, but now the torch is only a symbol.

The book she carries has a date on it: July 4, 1776—the date when the Declaration of

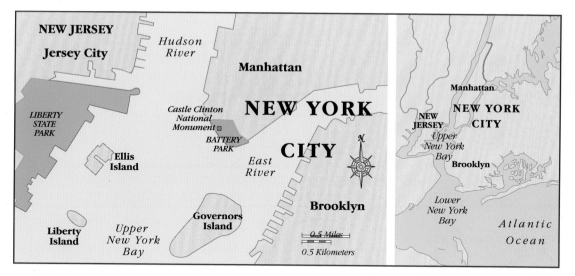

At the time the statue was placed on what is now called Liberty Island, New York Harbor was the busiest port in the United States. Nearby Ellis Island soon became the first stop for millions of immigrants coming to the United States.

Independence was approved and, in effect, the United States of America was born.

At the statue's feet are chains. These chains are a symbol of ideas that stop freedom. But the chains are broken. This means a free people can break through to find freedom. Also, the statue's right foot is lifted. It is as if she is going to take a step. She is moving beyond the chains into a life of freedom.

Seeing the Statue

Most Americans recognize the Statue of Liberty. They have seen pictures of it. Millions of small copies of the statue have been sold as souvenirs. Businesses use pictures of the statue in their advertising for everything from fruit to jeans. It is on stamps and posters and shows up in many movies. More than 3 million people, from all over the world, go to Liberty Island and visit the Statue of Liberty each year.

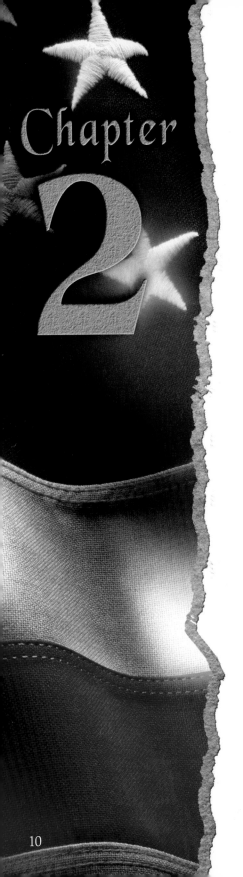

Chapter 2

A Gift Is Created

During the American Revolution, France sent soldiers and ships to help the American colonies defeat Great Britain. France and Great Britain were enemies at that time—each of them wanted to be the most powerful country in Europe. But the king of France did not decide to send help right away. Even before he did, other people in France decided to help the colonists because they believed in the ideas of freedom and democracy in the Declaration of Independence.

One of these people was the Marquis de Lafayette. He left France and came to America in 1777, and for the next two years he fought in the colonists' Continental Army. In 1779, Lafayette returned to France, and he helped convince the French government to send help to the colonists. The next year, he came back to America to continue fighting in the American Revolution. Americans were grateful to Lafayette, and he became a hero.

The Marquis de Lafayette (1757–1834)

Marie Jean Paul Joseph Roche Yves Gilbert du Motier, Marquis de Lafayette, was a rich French **noble**. He wanted France to have a republic like the new government that was set up in the United States after the American Revolution. After the French Revolution started in 1789, Lafayette worked for democracy in France, but except for short periods of time, France was not a democracy during his lifetime. In 1824, Congress invited him back to the United States for a visit. The U.S. government thanked him for fighting in the American Revolution and gave him land and money. When he returned to France, he took American dirt with him. He said he wanted to be buried in the "soil of America." He is still a symbol of the friendship between the two countries.

A revolution in France started in 1789, and soon after that the king of France was overthrown and killed. In the decades after the French Revolution, France had several governments. The French disagreed on what their government should be. Some people wanted it to again be a **monarchy**, led by a king. Others wanted a **republic**.

Edouard de Laboulaye was a French historian and expert on the American government. He wanted France's government to be more like that of the United States. In 1865, he talked with many people about having a French republic. Frédéric-Auguste Bartholdi agreed with him. Bartholdi was a **sculptor**. A sculptor is someone who creates art by making shapes, such as statues.

Bartholdi and Laboulaye talked about creating a statue. It would be a birthday gift from France to the United States for the 100th anniversary of the Declaration of Independence. It would honor the friendship between the two countries. Also, they hoped that the idea of the statue would get more people in France to support a French republic.

Laboulaye felt very strongly about the statue. Bartholdi wrote that he remembered Laboulaye saying:

> "If a monument were to be built in America as a memorial to their independence, I should think it very natural if it were built by united efforts, if it were a common work of both nations."

Bartholdi's American Visit

Laboulaye encouraged Bartholdi to visit the United States. In 1871, he did. When his ship arrived in New York Harbor, he saw where he wanted his great statue to stand. He wanted it on a small island that his ship was

Frédéric-Auguste Bartholdi (1834–1904)

Frédéric-Auguste Bartholdi was born in the Alsace region of France. In 1870–1871, he fought in the Franco-Prussian War. This was a war between France and Prussia (an area that is now part of Germany). After France was defeated in the war, it was forced to give Alsace to Prussia. This angered Bartholdi because the people in Alsace were not allowed to choose what country they wanted their region to be part of. This made Bartholdi value liberty even more than before. Bartholdi was a sculptor who liked to design large works of art.

In 1869, he designed a huge statue of a woman. It was to be built in Egypt. It would also be a lighthouse. But it was never built. Besides the Statue of Liberty, there are other works by Bartholdi in the United States, including a statue of Lafayette in New York City and a large fountain in Washington, D.C.

By the 1870s, when Bartholdi visited the United States, many Americans worked in factories. The workers here are in a factory that makes fabric.

passing. It would face toward the ocean and welcome people. Bartholdi later wrote, "In this very place shall be raised the Statue of Liberty, grand as the idea which it embodies [stands for]."

While he was in the United States, Bartholdi saw a country that was changing quickly. He visited growing cities, including Chicago. He loved American cities, where new factories and businesses opened every day. Thousands of people worked in them. Some Americans became very rich at this time. Millions more worked very hard for very little money. Sometimes children worked in factories, worked on farms, or made goods at home. Their families needed their help to survive. New railroads connected farms, factories, and cities. They carried raw materials and the growing amounts of manufactured goods that the country was making.

At a large workshop in Paris, workers made plaster models that were used to create the final copper statue.

Bartholdi was extremely excited about his statue and talked about it with people all over the United States. He even met with President Ulysses S. Grant. He told Americans that his statue would be a gift from the French people. Most people who heard about the statue liked the idea.

In 1875, Laboulaye and others in France set up an organization called the Franco-American Union. This group raised money to build Bartholdi's Statue of Liberty.

More than 180 French cities, large and small, gave money. Businesses and families gave, too. Some paid by going to special concerts or buying little statues. It took five years, but all of the money that was needed was raised. A month after the Franco-American Union began raising money, the French government approved a republican constitution—as Laboulaye had hoped, France now had a government like that of the United States.

Making Models

When Bartholdi returned from his trip to the United States, he began working on the statue. He made detailed drawings. He used some ideas from his earlier project, which never got made, for a huge statue in Egypt. Bartholdi said he thought of his mother's face as he designed the Statue of Liberty's face. He probably thought about how other artists had also shown liberty as a woman. He decided that his liberty would be peaceful. She would not have weapons.

First Bartholdi made a clay model of the statue that was 4 feet (1¼ meters) high. He made changes to it. Then he took it to the Paris workshop of a company that made artworks out of metal. This company had built other large statues.

Under Bartholdi's direction, workers at the company made a plaster model that was 9 feet (2¾ meters) high. With exact measurements, they made a third plaster that was 36 feet (11 meters) high. The workers then made thousands of measurements to make the pieces of a final plaster model that, if put together, would be the same size as the statue: 151 feet (46 meters) tall. (This last model was not put together, though. It would have been too tall to fit in the workshop.)

A Copper Skin

Following Bartholdi's directions, workers then built a wooden form around the outside of each piece of the final plaster model. They used small pieces of wood placed very close together. When they took off each form, the inside of the form was the same as the outside of that piece of the plaster model. Next, they pounded sheets of thin **copper** onto the inside of each wooden form. This was an old way of molding copper.

The wooden form used to create the statue's left hand was so large that workers could stand in it.

Bartholdi chose copper because it was thin but strong. Each of the 300 sheets of copper the workers used was about as thick as two pennies. These sheets were cut into shapes and then pounded into the wooden forms. Later, all of these molded copper pieces could be put together to make the copper "skin" that is the outside of the statue.

A Strong Frame

Bartholdi knew that the copper skin would need a strong frame inside it. He asked Alexandre-Gustave Eiffel to design it. Eiffel used modern methods to create a frame with three parts. Inside the center of the statue was a strong iron tower that would connect to the statue's base. Then, metal

Alexandre-Gustave Eiffel (1832–1923)

Alexandre-Gustave Eiffel was known for building large and strong railroad bridges using the newest methods, or technology. He used these same new ideas for the Statue of Liberty's frame. He is most famous for designing the Eiffel Tower (right). This steel and iron tower—984 feet (300 meters) tall—was built for the 1889 world's fair in Paris that celebrated the 100th anniversary of the start of the French Revolution. Until 1930, the Eiffel Tower was the tallest human-made structure in the world. When it was built, the Eiffel Tower was not meant to be permanent. But many people loved the tower's graceful beauty and the great views of Paris from the top. It is still in Paris today and is the most famous symbol of that city.

beams went out from that tower to the copper skin. These beams were attached to metal bars that went along the inside of the copper skin. This allowed each piece of the skin to be attached to a beam. With this kind of frame, the statue is able to adjust to the weather. It moves in the wind. When the weather is hot, the copper and metal bars expand, or get bigger. They contract, or get smaller, when the weather is cold.

Running Late

The whole statue was not ready in time for America's 100th birthday celebration in 1876. Instead, its arm and torch were sent to the United

When the statue was put up in Paris, it was taller than many of the city's buildings.

States and were shown at the 1876 Centennial Exhibition in Philadelphia. When the Exhibition closed, the torch was moved to Madison Square Park in New York City. It was there for two years. Then it returned to Paris. In Paris, in 1878, visitors paid to go into the statue's head.

Finally, in 1882, all the pieces of the statue were complete. Bartholdi and the workers put the statue together. First they built the iron frame outside the shop. Then they attached the copper skin to the frame. Soon, the statue towered over Paris. On July 4, 1884, a ceremony was held at the statue. People from the French and American governments were there. *Liberty Enlightening the World* was officially given to the United States. For the rest of the year the statue stayed in Paris. Many people came to see it.

Crossing the Atlantic

In January 1885, the statue was taken apart. Each of its hundreds of pieces was marked so that the statue could be rebuilt in New York. Then the

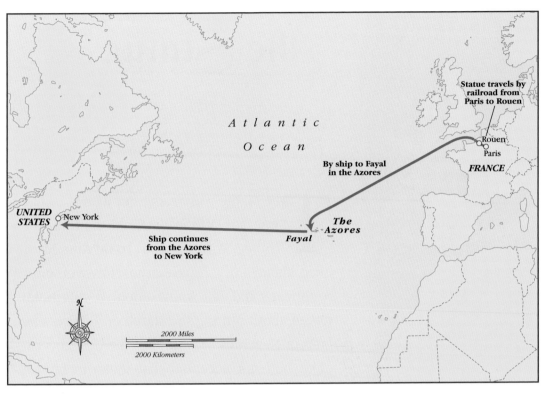

The statue had a rough journey across the Atlantic from France to New York. The ship carrying it ran into a severe storm before reaching its first stop in the Azores islands.

pieces went into 214 wooden boxes. All together the statue and the boxes weighed hundreds of thousands of pounds. Seventeen railroad cars took the boxes from Paris to the port at the city of Rouen. There, they were loaded onto a French warship, the *Isère*, for the long journey across the Atlantic Ocean to New York Harbor. A horrible storm caused very rough seas at the beginning of the trip. Then the ship ran out of coal and lost its steam power. It had to use its sails to continue the voyage. Some people were afraid that the statue would never make it to New York. Finally, on June 17, 1885, the ship arrived in New York Harbor. The statue's new home wasn't ready, though. The boxes were unloaded and stayed closed for another year. They just sat on Bedloe's Island.

Putting Up the Statue

The statue was ready, but its new home was not. When Bartholdi had left the United States in 1871, some Americans liked his idea of a huge statue. However, most Americans did not know about it. Bartholdi talked about putting the statue on Bedloe's Island in New York Harbor, but the U.S. government had not accepted that idea—in fact, it had not even officially said yes to the gift.

When the statue's torch came to the United States in 1876, most Americans began to take the gift seriously. Some people did not want it. They thought putting up and taking care of the statue would cost too much money. Others called it New York's lighthouse. They did not want anything to do with it. But some other cities said they would like to have it if New York did not want it. Cities including Philadelphia, Boston, and Cleveland said they would find a place for it.

In 1877, Congress finally voted to officially accept France's gift. Congress also agreed to make Bedloe's Island the statue's home and to pay for taking care of the statue after it was put up. But Congress refused to pay for building the **pedestal**, or base, on which the statue would stand.

Raising the Money for the Base

In 1877, a committee was formed to raise money to build the base. Big businesses and rich people gave money. Some people sold artworks they owned in order to raise money. In 1883, the American poet Emma Lazarus created a poem to help raise money. She believed the Statue of Liberty would be a good welcoming symbol for the many new immigrants who were starting to come to the United States at that time. Her poem, "The New Colossus," did not become famous until years later, though. Even with all of these efforts, the committee still did not have enough money. In 1883, work started anyway.

In 1885, the statue was finished in Paris. However, the work on Bedloe's Island had stopped. There just was not enough money to continue. It finally started again a few months later.

Bedloe's Island

Bedloe's Island is a small island in New York Harbor. Dutch colonists called it Oyster Island. For a while, Isaac Bedloe owned it. Later New York City sent very sick people to stay there. During the American Revolution, the buildings on the island were burned so that the Tories (Americans who remained loyal to Great Britain) could not use them. In 1800, New York State gave control of the island to the U.S. government, which built a fort there. The walls of the fort form a star with eleven points. The fort was used during the War of 1812 between the United States and Great Britain. Soon after, it was named Fort Wood to honor a hero in the war. The Statue of Liberty stands within the walls of the former fort.

The man who, perhaps, did more than anyone else to raise money for the statue's base was Joseph Pulitzer. He owned a New York City newspaper, *The World*. He liked the idea of the Statue of Liberty. He also wanted to sell more papers. He decided to use his newspaper to raise the rest of the money needed for the statue's base.

On March 16, 1885, he wrote a story for the paper. He asked people to send in money, and he promised to print the names of everyone who did, no matter how much or how little they sent. The paper kept printing stories about the statue. It wrote about the people who sent money. It told about children who collected money from customers of their fathers' businesses. Some children sent in their only dime. Clubs raised money. Immigrants sent money and told the paper how much the United States meant to them.

Joseph Pulitzer (1847–1911)

Joseph Pulitzer was a poor immigrant from Hungary who came to the United States in 1864. He fought in the Civil War (1861–1865). Then he moved to St. Louis. He started working at a newspaper, and soon he owned several newspapers. In 1883, he bought a New York newspaper, *The World*, and made it the most successful newspaper in the United States. Pulitzer became a very rich man. When he died, he left some of his money to be used for a series of special prizes. The Pulitzer Prizes are still given every year for the best reporting done by newspapers, for the best writing by **journalists** and other writers, and for the best work by photographers and music **composers**.

This newspaper showed a picture on its front page of the French ship *Isère* being greeted as it arrived in New York Harbor carrying the statue.

On April 1, 1885, the paper warned that the ship carrying the statue was leaving France. The money came in faster, but not fast enough. The paper was still raising money when the statue arrived in June. Finally, on August 11, 1885, the paper announced that it had raised the last $100,000 that was needed. It said that 125,000 people had sent in money.

Building the Pedestal

A lot of planning went into the pedestal. A committee was formed to do the planning. The people on the committee looked at many designs. A design by American **architect** Richard Morris Hunt was chosen. Hunt had studied in Paris and liked to use French styles in his designs. The pedestal he designed would be expensive to build, but it looked just right.

Much work had to be done before the pedestal could be built. Workers had to destroy some bomb-proof walls inside the fort. They had to bring

In Their Own Words

Pulitzer's Article in *The World*

This is part of Joseph Pulitzer's first article in *The World* about raising money for the Statue of Liberty:

"We must raise the money! *The World* is the people's paper, and it now appeals to [asks] the people to come forward and raise this money.... Let us not wait for the millionaires to give the money. It is not a gift from the millionaires of France to the millionaires of America.... Give something, however little. Send it to us. We will receive it.... We will also publish the name of every giver, however small the sum given. Let us hear from the people."

Part of the strong iron tower that would be inside the statue was attached to the base first, before workers started putting the copper skin around it.

In Their Own Words

President Cleveland Changes His Mind

Before he was president, Grover Cleveland was governor of New York. At that time, he did not seem to think that the Statue of Liberty was very important. He would not let New York City give money to build the pedestal. Later, as president, he opened the Statue of Liberty and gave a speech about how important it was. He said at the dedication:

"We will not forget that Liberty has here made her home; nor shall her chosen altar be neglected [forgotten].... A stream of light shall pierce the darkness of ignorance and man's oppression [injustice], until liberty enlightens the world."

supplies by ferry to Bedloe's Island. The ferry boat was called *Bartholdi*. A small railroad was built on the island. It helped move the heavy steel, **concrete**, and stone that was needed to the building site.

French and American teams worked on the pedestal. Like the statue, the pedestal used new technology. It had very thick walls made of concrete with steel in it to make it stronger. The steel itself was made very strong by a new process. Granite stone was placed around the outside of the base to make it look better. Workers added coins to the concrete to honor the people who gave money to put up the statue.

The pedestal is about as tall as a ten-story building. In fact, it is as tall as the statue itself. Some people were afraid that the statue would fall over. However, the base is so strong and heavy that this is not really possible. Inside the pedestal, stairs were built to take people to its top.

When the pedestal was finally ready in April 1886, the workers began opening the boxes that held the statue. They first attached the bottom of the iron tower that was part of Eiffel's frame to strong steel inside the pedestal. Next they attached the inside beams to the tower around the bottom. Then they attached the copper skin around the bottom. **Rivets** were used like nails to hold the pieces of copper skin together. The workers moved up the statue slowly. First they built part of the frame, and then they attached part of the skin.

The Americans made some changes to the statue as they put it up. Inside the statue, they added two spiral staircases for visitors to climb to the top. They changed the torch. They were afraid its light would be too bright. Finally, after four months of work, the statue had been completely put up on its base.

Parts of the feet and torch of the statue lie on the ground near the base before being lifted up and put in place.

On Dedication Day in 1886, New York Harbor was the scene of a huge celebration for the new Statue of Liberty. Ships blew their whistles, people waved flags, and there was a 21-gun salute.

In Their Own Words

A Dream Fulfilled

When Bartholdi saw the Statue of Liberty on Bedloe's Island, he said:

"The dream of my life is accomplished.... I see the symbol of unity and friendship between two nations—two republics."

Celebrating a Gift

October 28, 1886, was Dedication Day. Even though it rained, 20,000 people paraded through New York City. French and American flags were everywhere. New York Harbor was crowded with boats.

On Bedloe's Island, a French flag covered the statue's face. Invited guests heard speeches from President Grover Cleveland and others. The speakers talked about their love of the United States. They talked about liberty and friendship. They spoke about those who died for freedom.

Bartholdi was waiting for a special signal from someone on the ground. That person was to let him know when the speeches were over. But something happened. The signal was given too soon. Bartholdi pulled the rope while someone was still talking. When he pulled the rope, the French flag fell from the statue's face. Suddenly noise exploded everywhere. Foghorns blew. There was a 21-gun salute. Ships blew their whistles and sirens. People on the island, in boats, and on land began cheering.

Everyone was celebrating. For many it was just a party day. They did not really think the Statue of Liberty was anything special. It was not yet a special symbol. It was the tallest structure in the world. Soon, it would live up to its name: *Liberty Enlightening the World.*

The Next 100 Years

In the next 25 years or so after 1886, more than 12 million immigrants entered the United States through New York Harbor. As their ships came into the harbor, they saw the Statue of Liberty. To them, she was the symbol of the United States. She stood for the place where they hoped they would find freedom and opportunity and could build a new life. As one immigrant from that time said:

> "We just gazed on it. We couldn't really grasp the meaning of it, but it was a very penetrating [deep] feeling to see that symbol of freedom."

Emma Lazarus's poem about the statue was coming true. She had called immigrants "huddled masses yearning to breathe free." More and more of them were coming to the United States. In 1903 a **bronze plaque** with her poem on it was added to the inside of the base of the statue. The poem became popular

For the statue's 100th birthday, there was another huge celebration. Here, fireworks light the night sky over New York Harbor on July 3, 1986.

during World War II (1939–1945). At that time, much of the world was fighting for freedom.

The statue was more than a symbol. People came to visit it. They climbed the stairs inside the statue to the crown and the torch and looked out at New York. The statue was also a lighthouse at this time and was run by a U.S. government agency called the United States Lighthouse Board. The lighthouse keeper lived on Bedloe's Island. But the statue's light was never strong enough to shine very far. The island's Fort Wood remained a military base. In 1902, the War Department took control of the statue.

World War I—Land of the Free

During World War I people began to see the Statue of Liberty in a new way. The war started in Europe in 1914, and it involved many countries. Three of the largest countries fighting were Great Britain and France, on one side, against Germany, on the other side. Great Britain and France were countries in which people had a great deal of freedom.

As the war continued, Americans raised money to make the lights on the Statue of Liberty brighter. They wanted to show that the United

States was shining the light of liberty brighter than ever. In 1916, Gutzon Borglum, who later carved Mount Rushmore, was chosen to change the torch. He cut away most of the copper on the flame and replaced it with 250 pieces of yellowish glass. He put an electric light inside it. It was still not very bright, though.

The United States joined World War I in 1917, on the side of Britain and France. The U.S. government used the Statue of Liberty as a symbol of freedom. Many Americans had never seen the statue. Suddenly, posters with its picture were everywhere. By the end of the war, most Americans knew what the statue looked like and thought of it as a symbol of liberty.

During the war, a huge explosion was set by men working for Germany. It blew up a New Jersey shipping area, Black Tom Wharf. The blast was so strong that it was felt at the statue. After that, the torch was closed to visitors. After the war, American soldiers returning from Europe sailed into

New York Harbor. They cheered when they saw Lady Liberty. To them, the statue represented home and freedom. To the rest of the world, the statue was becoming more and more famous as a symbol of the United States. More people came to visit the statue. In 1924, the U.S. government decided to make the Statue of Liberty and Fort Wood a national monument.

The Statue of Liberty's 1916 torch, with its 250 pieces of yellow glass, can now be seen inside the base of the statue.

Liberty Bonds

After the United States entered World War I, the U.S. government sold "Liberty Bonds." The money people paid to buy the bonds was used to pay for the war. Posters asked Americans to buy these bonds. To get people interested, they used symbols. They showed soldiers and nurses. They showed the flag and Uncle Sam. They also used the Statue of Liberty. Some posters reminded immigrants that they came to the United States for freedom. A lot of money was raised in this way.

One of the many World War I posters urging people to buy Liberty Bonds that featured the Statue of Liberty.

The Statue Turns 50

In the 1930s, President Franklin D. Roosevelt hired many people who were out of work at the time to do government jobs. Some worked on Bedloe's Island. The old Army buildings were destroyed. The statue was closed to make repairs. The torch, the frame, the stairs, and the spikes in the crown were fixed. In 1933, the National Park Service began running the statue, and four years later all of Bedloe's Island became part of the Statue of Liberty National Monument.

In 1936, the statue turned 50 years old. The Park Service planned a celebration. President Roosevelt gave a speech at the statue and spoke about the immigrants who had come to the United States: "Here they found life because here there was freedom to live." This was an important message at that time. Many people in Europe were losing their freedom to **dictatorships** that wanted to take over other countries.

In Their Own Words

"The New Colossus"

This is the poem, "The New Colossus," that Emma Lazarus wrote in 1883:

Not like the brazen giant of Greek fame,
With conquering limbs astride from land to land
Here at our sea-washed, sunset gates shall stand
A mighty woman with a torch, whose flame
Is the imprisoned lightning, and her name
Mother of Exiles. From her beacon-hand
Glows world-wide welcome; her mild eyes command
The air-bridged harbor that twin cities frame.
"Keep, ancient lands, your storied pomp!" cries she
With silent lips. "Give me your tired, your poor,
Your huddled masses, yearning to breathe free,
The wretched refuse of your teeming shore.
Send these, the homeless, tempest-tost, to me;
I lift my lamp beside the golden door!"

The Statue in World War II

The United States joined World War II in 1941. It fought around the world against the armies of the dictatorships of Germany and Japan. This time the government turned off the lights at the Statue of Liberty. They stayed off to save electricity. The lights came back on only twice during the war. The first time was for 15 minutes on D-Day, June 6, 1944. That was the day tens of thousands of American, British, and other soldiers landed in France to fight against Germany, which had taken over France earlier in the war. The second time was on VE Day, the day in 1945 when the war ended in Europe. The war in Asia ended a few months later, completely ending World War II. Germany and Japan had been defeated. Soon after, military ships bringing American soldiers home again passed the statue. Again, the soldiers cheered for the statue, for their country, and for liberty.

More Popular Than Ever

The number of visitors to the Statue of Liberty continued to grow. Guides told the story of Bartholdi and the building of the statue. In 1956, the name of Bedloe's Island was officially changed to Liberty Island. In 1972, the American Museum of Immigration opened. It told how immigration was important to American history. It closed in 1991 because a new museum on immigration had opened nearby at Ellis Island.

In 1976, the United States celebrated the 200th anniversary of the Declaration of Independence. Part of the celebration was in New York Harbor near the statue. On July 4, 1976, a parade of tall sailing ships glided past her while many more boats floated in the harbor. That night, fireworks lit the sky all around the statue.

Getting Ready for 100

In 1982, the Statue of Liberty-Ellis Island Foundation was started. Both places needed to be restored, or fixed up. The statue was to be fixed by 1986, when it turned 100 years old.

Once again, Americans were asked to give money—this time to restore what

In the 1980s, the statue was repaired and cleaned in preparation for its 100th birthday.

people's gifts had earlier helped to build. Millions of people gave money, and so did many businesses, large and small. Hundreds of millions of dollars were raised.

Architects were hired to restore the statue. For two years they examined the statue. They studied Bartholdi's and Eiffel's plans. They even studied the weather at the statue.

A huge **scaffold** was put up around the statue. A scaffold is a frame for workers to stand on while building or fixing something. This scaffold was planned very carefully. It did not touch the statue, even during hurricane winds. Yet, it was strong enough to hold a large, heavy crane that was needed to bring down the torch for repairs.

Once the scaffold was up, the workers found birds' nests and cracks in the statue. They found written on the statue the names of people who had worked on it earlier. They even found a B for Bartholdi on the first copper plate that was riveted when the statue was first put up.

When workers took down the torch, they found that it leaked. The architects decided to make a new torch and used Bartholdi's original design. Workers even made it in the same way as Bartholdi's workers had made the first torch.

After the statue got a good washing, the workers saw that most of the copper skin was in good shape. The statue had turned green by this time,

Happy 100th Birthday

On July 3, 1986, the Statue of Liberty reopened. President Ronald Reagan spoke at a ceremony at the statue and lit the statue's lights. The birthday celebration lasted for three days. Fireworks, a parade of tall ships, speeches, and picnics took place in and around New York Harbor. Lady Liberty entered her second hundred years in a grand way.

and this green **patina** that had formed on the copper had protected it. Workers replaced rivets and closed cracks and tears. The spikes on the crown were taken off and cleaned. The raised arm was fixed.

The workers had to clean and fix the inside of the statue, too. They washed the inside and took off many layers of paint. They cleaned and repaired Eiffel's frame, replacing 1,350 bars along the copper skin. This had to be done quickly so the copper would not change shape. They made sure that the rest of the frame was still strong and that the copper skin was tightly attached to it. They replaced the steps.

The concrete and stone in the pedestal needed very little work. Workers did add new doors and a new elevator. The new torch was raised. It was copper and the flame was covered in gold. Sun-

Crew members on this ship from the country of Colombia honor the statue as they sail by during Lady Liberty's 100th birthday celebration.

shine and spotlights make it shine day and night. Many of the workers who repaired the statue were very proud to be part of the effort to help restore such an important symbol.

5

Visiting the Statue Today

Most people agree that the Statue of Liberty is very special. In 1984, UNESCO, a part of the United Nations, named it a World Heritage Site. This means it is a place that is important to people all over the world.

More than 3 million people—Americans and people from many other countries—visit the statue every year. Some buy their tickets in advance, over the Internet. Anyone who wants to go inside the pedestal must have a ticket. Tickets for the day often sell out early in the morning.

Most people going to Liberty Island take a ferry from Battery Park in Manhattan. They buy their tickets at Castle Clinton. This was once Castle Garden, a place where for many years immigrants entered the United States before Ellis Island was opened for that purpose. Today, displays at Castle Clinton tell its history.

A ferry arrives at Liberty Island with a boat full of visitors.

Other people take a ferry from New Jersey's Liberty State Park. This area was once the site of a train station, and then it was used as a dump. Today it is a beautiful state park.

Before boarding a ferry, visitors must go through a security check. The National Park Service uses security checks to try to keep special places like the statue safe. From either Manhattan or New Jersey, the ferry ride to Liberty Island is short. Most people spend the ride looking at the New York City skyline and Lady Liberty. They can see the statue as Bartholdi meant it to be seen, from the water.

The Outside Tour

Liberty Island is not very big. It has only a few buildings and the statue on it. The Park Rangers have an office there. Rangers give tours of the island.

Many visitors just walk around Liberty Island. They enjoy looking up at the statue. They look across to the New York City skyline and to New Jersey. Some rent an audio tour. With headsets, they listen to the history of Liberty Island and learn about the building of the Statue of Liberty.

A path follows the outside of Fort Wood. Along it are five small statues of the most important people in the statue's life: Laboulaye, Bartholdi, Eiffel, Pulitzer, and Lazarus. All along the path are signs that tell about the history of the statue.

From inside the base, visitors can see this spiral staircase that goes up to the statue's crown.

Inside the Pedestal

Those who have tickets to the pedestal go through another security check. Inside the pedestal is a museum about the statue. The first thing you see is the old torch. This torch was not put back on the statue in 1986 because it was not strong enough. Water had damaged it, so a new one was built. There is also a full-sized copy of the statue's face.

Going to the Top

Until 2001, visitors to the statue could climb the spiral staircase inside it and go into Lady Liberty's crown. From windows in the crown, they could enjoy great views of New York City, New Jersey, and the harbor. After terrorists attacked the United States on September 11, 2001, the National Park Service closed the staircase to the crown, to make sure visitors to the statue would be safe. (Even the pedestal was closed for a time.) In the spring of 2009, the government said it was safe for visitors to go up to the crown. Starting on July 4, 2009, a small number of people would be allowed to climb the spiral staircase each day.

Statue Statistics

Here are some of the many amazing facts about the Statue of Liberty:

Height of the statue (to the tip of the torch):	151'1"	46.05 m
Height of the base:	154'0"	46.94 m
Total height of the statue and base (from the ground to the tip of the torch):	305'1"	92.99 m
Height from the heel to the top of head:	111'1"	33.86 m
Height of the head:	17'3"	5.26 m
Width of each eye:	2'6"	0.76 m
Length of the nose:	4'6"	1.37 m
Length of the raised right arm:	42'0"	12.80 m
Weight of the statue's copper skin:	62,000 lbs.	28,123 kg
Weight of statue's steel frame:	250,000 lbs.	113,398 kg
Weight of the concrete in the base:	27,000 tons	24,494 metric tons

One section of the museum tells what immigrants thought of the statue. This is where visitors can see the plaque with Emma Lazarus's poem.

Up the Pedestal

From the museum, visitors can walk up 156 steps inside the pedestal. Looking up, they can see inside the statue—Eiffel's frame, the bars that hold

Ellis Island

Opened in 1892, Ellis Island was the most important immigration center in the United States for the next 32 years. From 1892 to 1924, more than 12 million immigrants came to Ellis Island. Most immigrants quickly passed the medical and other tests given there. They left and went to New York City or New Jersey. Many stayed in the New York area, and many others took trains to places all over the United States. If they were sick, immigrants stayed on the island. Some were sent back to the country they came from. Ellis Island was closed in 1954. In 1982, the Statue of Liberty-Ellis Island Foundation raised money to restore it. In 1990, it opened as a museum, and now it tells the story of the people who went through Ellis Island.

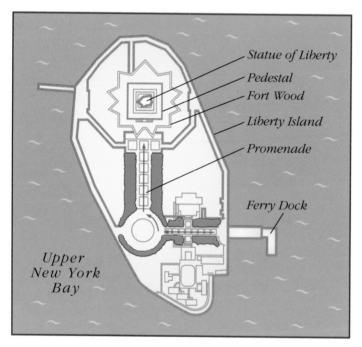

Statue of Liberty

Pedestal

Fort Wood

Liberty Island

Promenade

Ferry Dock

Upper New York Bay

After leaving the ferry, visitors have a short walk to the pedestal, or they can simply walk around Liberty Island.

the copper skin, and the spiral staircase that leads to the crown.

After climbing the pedestal's stairs, visitors can go outside and walk around on the top of the pedestal. There are great views of New York and New Jersey. Someone looking up from the top of the pedestal cannot see the whole statue. You can see the folds of her dress, the bottom of her torch, and the spikes on her crown.

Still a symbol of American freedom, the Statue of Liberty is lit up each evening as she stands in New York Harbor.

You cannot see her feet, face, or flame. After going back down the steps and going outside again, visitors can walk along the inside of Fort Wood's star-shape.

The End of the Visit

To leave, visitors again take the ferry. Before going back to either Manhattan or New Jersey, the boat will stop at Ellis Island. From 1892 to 1924 most of the immigrants entering the United States first went to Ellis Island. In 1965, it became part of the Statue of Liberty National Monument. Today, Ellis Island is a museum. It tells the story of the immigrants who entered the United States at New York.

From the ferry heading back, visitors can again see Lady Liberty. In 1886, *Liberty Enlightening the World* was a symbol of friendship. To the French, she was also a symbol of the American republic. She was a symbol of freedom and opportunity to millions of immigrants. Today, she is still a symbol of freedom and friendship. To the whole world, she is a symbol of the United States of America.

Timeline ★ ★ ★ ★ ★ ★ ★ ★

★ **1811**   A fort is built on Bedloe's Island in New York Harbor. It is later named Fort Wood.

★ **1865**   Edouard de Laboulaye and Frédéric-Auguste Bartholdi of France discuss a gift to the United States.

★ **1871**   Bartholdi visits the United States and picks Bedloe's Island as the site for his statue.

★ **1875**   Laboulaye begins raising money for the statue in France.

★ **1876**   Bartholdi shows the statue's torch and arm at a Centennial Exhibition in Philadelphia.

★ **1877**   The U.S. Congress agrees to accept the statue as a gift.

★ **1879**   Alexandre-Gustave Eiffel designs the statue's frame.

★ **1882**   Bartholdi completes all of the pieces of the statue and begins putting it together in Paris.

★ **1883**   Work starts on Bedloe's Island to build the base.

★ **1885**   The statue is taken apart and shipped to New York. In the United States, newspaper owner Joseph Pulitzer raises money to finish building the base.

★ **1886**   The base is completed, and the statue is put together on Bedloe's Island. **October 28:** The statue opens on Dedication Day.

★ **1903**   Emma Lazarus's poem is placed in the base.

★ **1924**   The Statue of Liberty is made a national monument.

★ **1933**   The National Park Service takes control of running the Statue of Liberty.

★ **1956**   Bedloe's Island is renamed Liberty Island.

★ **1986**   Work to restore the statue is completed in time for a celebration for her 100th birthday.

★ **2001**   The statue closes because of the September 11 terrorist attacks. Liberty Island reopens in December.

★ **2004**   The pedestal and the museum inside it are reopened.

★ **2009**   The staircase to the statue's crown is reopened for a small number of visitors each day.

architect: A person who designs buildings and other structures and who understands how they are built.

bronze: A metal made mostly of copper and tin.

composer: A person who writes music.

concrete: A combination of cement (a mix of crushed limestone and clay), pebbles, sand, and water that dries very hard.

copper: A reddish-brown metal that can easily be formed into shapes.

dedicated: Opened with a ceremony or a celebration.

democracy: A form of government in which power is held by all the people, who usually choose leaders to make laws and run the government for them.

dictatorship: A form of government in which the government leader or leaders hold all power and allow very little freedom.

immigrant: Someone from one country who moves to another country to live permanently.

journalist: A person who reports news for a newspaper or magazine, on television or radio, on the Internet, or in some other way.

lighthouse: A large tower with a light that guides ships, usually away from shallow water or rocks.

monarchy: A government headed by a king or queen, who usually has a great deal of power.

noble: A person, often wealthy, who is a member of the upper classes; the noble or the noble's family may own a large amount of land.

patina: The green coating that forms on copper when wet air hits the metal over a long period of time.

pedestal: The base or support at the bottom of something.

plaque: A flat, thin piece of metal or wood with writing on it.

republic: A country with a government in which people vote for the leaders who make their laws and run the government.

rivet: A rod with a head on one end used to fasten things together; the rod is inserted in a hole and, when in place, the other end is hit to create another head to hold the rod in place.

scaffold: A metal or wooden frame put up to hold workers while building or fixing something, often at great heights.

sculptor: A person who creates art by making shapes, like statues, often out of metal or stone.

symbol: Something that stands for something else, often an idea or a place.

To Learn More ★ ★ ★ ★ ★ ★

Read these books

Ashley, Susan. *The Statue of Liberty*. Milwaukee: Gareth Stevens, 2004.

Curlee, Lynn. *Liberty*. New York: Scholastic, 2003.

Hochain, Serge. *Building Liberty*. Des Moines, Iowa: National Geographic, 2004.

Moreno, Barry. *Statue of Liberty*. Mount Pleasant, S.C.: Arcadia Publishing, 2004.

Niz, Xavier, and Cynthia Martin. *The Story of the Statue of Liberty*. Mankato, Minn.: Capstone, 2006.

Rappaport, Doreen. *Lady Liberty: A Biography*. Somerville, Mass.: Candlewick, 2008.

Silate, Jennifer. *The Statue of Liberty*. New York: Rosen Publishing, 2006.

Look up these Web sites

The Light of Liberty
http://www.nationalgeographic.com/ngkids/9907/liberty/index.html

Meet the People
http://www.nps.gov/archive/stli/teachercorner/page4.html

Statue of Liberty Junior Ranger Program Activity Guide
http://www.nps.gov/stli/forkids/index.htm

Statue of Liberty Official Website
http://www.nps.gov/stli

Statue of Liberty Resources
http://www.statueofliberty.org/default_sol.htm

Key Internet search terms

Frédéric-Auguste Bartholdi, Alexandre-Gustave Eiffel, Ellis Island, immigrants, Edouard de Laboulaye, Statue of Liberty

The abbreviation *ill.* stands for illustration, and *ills.* stands for illustrations. Page references to illustrations and maps are in *italic* type.

Index ★ ★ ★ ★ ★ ★ ★ ★ ★

★ ★

About the Author

Hilarie Staton has written for students and teachers for more than twenty-five years. She enjoys researching and writing about history, especially using original documents. She lives in the Hudson Valley in New York, an area where she finds many American history stories to tell. Other books about history she has written include *The Progressive Party: The Success of a Failed Party*.